I Still Remember the Last Time You Held My Hand

DAVID GIVER

I Still Remember the Last Time You Held My Hand

Copyright © 2015 by David Giver

All rights reserved. No part of this book may be reproduced or transmitted in any form or by any means without written permission of the author.

Library of Congress Control Number: 2015951748

ISBN: 978-0-9907958-7-2

Published by Shabda Press
Pasadena, CA 91107
www.shabdapress.com

I dedicate this to my daughter, the light of my life.

Table of Contents

I. 1
II. 27
III. 41
IV. 77
V. 107
VI. 115

I.

This next part is in dispute
As it matters whom you ask as to what happened
Felipe claims it was his master that pulled them
Onto the ice-covered water
And it was this move that caused them
To fall through the ice and into the frigid
wintry water,
But his master, the only one with a working
Knowledge of discernible English
Claims, and continues to claim,

As he says, on his dead mother's grave,
That it was that damned dog, Felipe, who so obviously
Hates him
That pulled him onto the frozen lake
And it was because of the dog
And the dog alone
That they plunged into the lake

As if they were practicing
For some damned charity event
In which people pay, and raise money,
To be tortured in such a way

Still holding onto the dog's leash
He pulled the dog's nearly lifeless
Body back up to the surface
And with one hand pressed against its chest
And the other under its ass, its tail wedged securely
Between its legs
He pushed Felipe
(That damned dog)
Back onto the ice, and back toward the shore line
With its rocky, imperfect horizon

Felipe just shook off the water
Hair matted to his shivering pink skin
And stared back at his master,
No longer loyal
To the man who attempted to kill them both
Allegedly
At least according to Felipe's testimony
Which he would give to any schnauzer or tea cup poodle
That would listen
And unlike the story his master would
Give to both the police officer and later, his wife,
About struggling to remove his dying body from the depths
Of that icy grave

As he emerged, he could hear the siren
Of the village's single police car
Alerting the whole world to his
Less than courageous exploits
Though he would grow in valor
With each personal telling
Of his heroic saving
Of poor, beloved Felipe
An anonymous 911 call had come in
About a man and his dog crashing through the ice
Anonymous it was not
As old Mrs. Lawrence
That gossipy old sow
Her binoculars close by her bed
Uncased on the bedside table
The two dustless spots of the table
Two perfect rings
Home to
The vulcanized rubber membranes
That gently caress the perfectly round
Lenses
Has the only home with a view
Of that part of the lake
And she prides herself
On her selfless vigilance
Anonymous as it was that anonymity
Would only hold until lunch
When the flood waters would rise over
The dam (mouth) of Lawrence
And the gossip would spread
Like wildfire

But the officer was nice enough to continue the ruse
Though no one was sure as to who was being fooled
As both parties
Knew the voice from the other end
Of the receiver

Officer Bouchard rushed to the lake's edge
With towels and blankets
Personally drying off, and wrapping up,
Poor, frozen Felipe
Even though he was the alleged cause of the debacle
The dog was being treated as victim
Much to its master's chagrin
As he would repeat
Repeatedly
That it was that damned dog
The one that so obviously loathes him
That was the cause of its own
Near demise
And that if he had not jumped in
All would have been lost
And there would have been
No dog to dry off

Dried as much as could be expected on such
A cold morning
The two, master and beast,
Slid across the hard plastic bench of the police cruiser
Not even a cushion
Which would be explained away
As necessary
As one never knew the state
Of those being assigned to that back bench
Be they bleeding
Disease washing all over the interior
Or a bit too inebriated to hold down
What he had had for lunch
As cleaning vomit
Out of upholstery
Was of no fun to anyone
And so
They took the ride home
Pleading with Bouchard to silence the siren
But being told it was necessary
Felipe arrived home to fanfare
Fanfare that the man did not also enjoy
As he was shamed by his wife and child
Both of whom had appeared on the porch
By the time the cruiser came to a stop
In front of the two-story Victorian
Home that needed a few coats of new paint

The boy, Izzy, jumped from the porch
His fleece robe catching the wind and floating straight out behind him
Ran toward the cruiser
Past his father

And wrapped his tiny arms around Felipe's neck
His father realizing that this was the nicest welcome he could expect
Plodded further up the sidewalk
And past the disapproving glance of his wife
And through the still ajar front door

Just as he crossed the threshold
Officer Bouchard called to him that there may be
Paperwork to file later
And that he would be in touch

This is when he noticed that his wife
Who he had thought to still be on the front porch
Was in fact directly behind him

"quite the run this morning"
"yes, it was a great run, Rachel!"
"don't be a smart ass"
"I am not being a smart ass"
"yes, you are"
"whatever ... can I get out of these wet clothes. Is that possible?"
"this isn't over"
"it never is"
"you are doing it again"
"doing what, again"
"you know"
"being a smart ass?"
"exactly"

He stripped down to his skin
Flung the clothes into the hamper
And turned on the shower

"is that for Felipe?"
Came a voice from the bottom of the stairs
Screaming back in the same direction
"is what for Felipe?"
"the shower"
"yes, Rachel, I was getting the shower ready for Felipe"
"you don't have to be an ass"
"what?"
"stop being an ass. It was just a question"

Standing naked, and shivering
He decided to be done with this conversation
And stepped into the steamy shower
Which even though it felt like pins and needles
Against his cold epidermis
It was bliss
The one happy moment of his morning
That is until
Felipe rubbed against his leg

"you said it was for him"
Rachel said with a joy he knew all too well
"thanks, Rachel, thanks"
"don't thank me, it was your idea"
He exited the shower as gracefully as one can
With an enormous wet dog blocking the natural path out
Wrapping the towel around his waist
He was stopped for further interrogation

"so what happened at the lake"
"do you really fucking care?"
"of course, I care"
"about me or the dog"
"you"
"bullshit"
"fine… the dog"
"just be honest"
"so what happened?"
"we ran to the lake, as usual"
"and your damned dog pulled us out onto the ice"
"my damned dog"
"do you want to hear the story or not?"
"I do"
"well, your damned dog pulled us out onto the ice
And it must have been weak where we were standing
As we fell through as soon as I could get him to stop"
"how long was he under?"
"I am fine, thanks"
"how long was he under?"
"just a few seconds. I pulled him out first
And pushed him back to shore"

She hugged him
It felt foreign
It was foreign
This was probably the first hug she had given him
In the last six months
And while it did feel nice
It was not because he had come home safely
It was because, like she would have, he had
Put Felipe first, had thought to get Felipe
Out of the lake first

The hug lingered more than he had felt comfortable with
Especially after coming to the conclusion
Of its impetus
But it soon ended
And she excused herself to the bathroom
To get Felipe from the shower
And to dry him off

He went to work
A job that he had taken right out of college
Not because it was the future he had always hoped for
Rather because Rachel came home one day
After work
And told him they needed to talk
They were just months away from graduation
And he was sure that she had finally seen him
For the phony he felt like
Whenever he walked arm in arm with her
Through the streets
The heads turned to see how it was that such a man could have such a woman
It oscillated between the facts that he must be well off
Financially, that he must be of family money, or
A silicon valley millionaire
Or what seemed to be the more likely
Unless you knew his anatomy
Like his doctor did
Which was to say that the passerby
Imagined that to be with a woman like Rachel
With the looks and demeanor that the man
So honestly possessed
That he must be well endowed
Not only well endowed, but also
An illusionist, as no endowment was visible
To the naked eye

She needed to talk to him
And knowing that it was best to confront him
In public spaces
As he would be less likely to explode or freak out
She invited him to Giacomo's
A local dive pizza place
A place very similar to the one they had met at
Though that one went
By another ethnically Italian name
They ordered their food
And as they waited, neither touched on her need to talk
Both hoping to wait it out
That if they did not speak
It would just happen and they could move on

But Rachel spoke
Of how it was such a beautiful spring day
How she wished they could all be like this
Not too hot, not too cold
Maybe everyday could be this way
He said that would be nice
Hoping that being kind would make this issue easier to get through
Taking a long gulp of water
Settling deeper into her seat
Clearing her throat slightly
Rachel spoke of the fact that she was late
He knew not what she was late for
As she was a rather punctual woman
And he told her so
To which she grimaced
And said in more clear and concise terms
That she was with child
That she was pregnant
But when either of them retells the story
She says that she was with child
And they usually pick a nicer venue than Giacomo's
And they gloss over the fact that it was chosen to limit
His possible reaction

"are you sure?"
"am I sure?"
"yes, are you sure?"
"of course, I am sure"
"so you have seen a doctor"
"no, but it does not take a doctor to be pregnant"

The conversation ended with the decision
That they should be sure
That they should see a doctor
As while it did not take one to get pregnant
It sure was helpful to double check with one to guarantee
The accuracy of a three dollar test from the pharmacy around the corner

Three days and a doctor's visit later
They were pregnant
Though he fought that terminology
As he felt as though it gave him too much credit
She fought back
And won
So they were pregnant
And were happy
But who to tell
They wanted to tell someone
That is, besides the doctor
But that had been unfair, as the doctor only knew out of necessity
Not out of celebration

They decided on his older sister, Mary
As she had just had a child, a daughter
And Rachel had no siblings
For if she had
The decision would have been made easier
But Mary won out over Rachel's mother
Because unconsciously
Neither wanted to deal with the argument/conversation
That would come from a baby out of wedlock
So Mary received a call at 8:13 a.m. on Wednesday
A bit early for her
But as late as Rachel could wait
And while Mary was happy for the pair
They had miscalculated her openness to their current relationship status
And the conversation that they were hoping to postpone
Until the happiness and joy of celebration had washed over them
For at least a short while
Came crashing upon them
Before smiles had even cracked their lips
Unhappy about this unplanned excursion
He hung up on his sister
To which Rachel decided there needed to be further punctuation
To the hurt felt in his heart

"I told you we should have called my mother"
"what?"
"I told you"
"you said we should tell someone else to be able to be happy
Before such awkward conversations were to follow
And while it did not go according to plan
You never said that we should just call your mother first
No matter the consequence"
"I did too"
"whatever"

He left the room
The apartment
And the street
And was on his way to the library
When he received a phone call from his mother
Asking if it was true
And why was she hearing this news from his girlfriend
And not him
He apologized and told her that he had wanted to tell her that Rachel was pregnant
But they had a plan

"what do you mean she is pregnant?"
"what do you mean, what do I mean?"
"she said you two were engaged"
"what?"
"yeah… and that the wedding would be around the time of graduation
To have everyone around"
"oh, right"

There was a long pause
A pregnant pause
One that said more
Than it didn't say
Speaking of his mother's hurt
Of his fiancé's betrayal
Of a future in flux
Confusion

"so she is pregnant?"
"yes, mom, she is pregnant
we found out yesterday"
"it is not ideal"
"I know, mom"
"but at least you are getting married"
"right"

He lied and told his mother that Rachel was on the other line
To which his mother said take your soon to be bride's call
And that they were excited about all of the new news
Even though he knew his father would need to be eased into it
So the excitement was solely that of his mother
As soon as the line was free
He dialed his bride to be
And they screamed at each other
For the better part of three city blocks
Before he was defeated
And went silent
To which she said they would talk later
And he continued onto the library

Where he tried to write the paper on Rawls' Theory of Justice
Thinking of what might be ahead of him
Thinking of what they had planned together
Prior to this addendum
Was now gone
And what would the future hold

He grabbed a cup of coffee on the way home
From the library,
and began to think of how he was going to support this new family
Which was also on the mind of Rachel
As she had for him,
when he came through the door
A name and number of a family friend
That managed the local branch
Of some national bank
And how he had a low-level management job
That would be perfect
And not wanting to look
He took the number
Called the gentleman
Who asked him a couple of questions over the phone
And then said the job was his
If he wanted it
(He didn't)
And that they would work with his schedule
At university
And that after graduation
He would move to a steady 40-hour a week schedule
Resigned,
he took the job
And thanked the gentleman

That was eight years ago
And while he had moved up at the bank
And was making a good salary
And had a great company paid insurance
And 401(k) plan
He loathed his life

Tightening his tie tight against his Adam's apple
Wanting to feel
He jumped in the sedan (black) that he was told
Was perfect for a man of his status
By the dealer
A man he had never met before
And drove off to the bank
Which was abuzz with the early morning
Incident that was the cause for his tardiness
A tardiness that was new for him
As he had not been late in those eight years at the bank

He walked quietly to his office
Feigning aloofness
Hoping that if he seemed over it
That others would get over it too
This proved a failure
As just as his ass met his chair
In came Roger
All agog about how the dog had gotten the best of him
And he defended the dog
Though he despised the dog
Knowing that not even Felipe would believe this
When he would hear it later
As Rachel commenced on her daily interrogation
Followed by a less than appetizing dinner

Roger finally reached the end of his comedic monologue
The office emptied
And the day's work continued unperturbed
Mortgage numbers
Profit and loss reports
Meeting after morose meeting
All talking about the same things
Just in different dialects

His bones still aching from the morning's
Ice cold water
He reached to pick up the receiver
Of the phone
On his desk
It was Rachel
She was scared, concerned, frightened
About Felipe
And how he had not stopped
Shivering
Even after the nice hot shower
And the drying off
With a towel, the warmth
Of the dryer still on it
And the blow out that she performed
When his teeth would not stop chattering
This litany was passing through his ears
And out into the vacant space of the office
As he imagined Rachel caring for him
In such a manner

Recalling a spring day
Years ago when the April showers
Came on schedule, but not on forecast
And the two were caught in the deluge
Taking cover under the abandoned marquee
Of the Mirage theater
A grand old movie house that had no further
Use these days than cover from a storm
And he made a break for the car
Two blocks away
Becoming drenched to the bone
His clothes becoming his skin
Like an attempt at making a papier-mâché
Body double

The door open
The wetness on his person permeating
The cloth upholstery of his late
Model Toyota
And as he turned the key in the ignition
As if by miracle
But surely happenstance
The rain ceased

Returning to the Mirage
He found his date exactly where
He had left her
A smile that obscured the rest of her face
Greeted him
As she entered the car; dry
And asking why he was so wet
He grinned
Knowing no good could come from sharing his feelings
Even though Rachel always claimed
To want honest communication
He smiled
Kissed her cheek
Placed the car into gear, and head off home
Where he was offered
And accepted
A couple's shower
Rachel's gentle skin grazing his
As she soaped up his body
Leaving no nook
Nor cranny unwashed
He felt loved. She toweled him off
And the duo made love
With a connection that felt new
And now --
Outside of the love making
As he felt Rachel
While she loved Felipe
Was not a practitioner
Of bestiality --
Felipe received that treatment
That connection
And had Felipe wore clothes
He could only imagine hearing
The buzzer of the dryer go off in the distance
As he held the receiver closer
In the hopes of maybe re-entering the conversation

Without divulging he had spaced out
Success

He returned just in time to hear that Rachel
Was on her way to Dr. Hall
Felipe's veterinarian
As this must be dealt with immediately, and that he must
Go to the school by 4
To pick up Izzy
He agreed
Realized that he could not
But Rachel had already left the line
And no matter how he tried
He could not get her back
Causing him to wonder if she did this to all callers
Or just to him
Or just when she wanted him to do things
Knowing he would agree
Even if impossible for him to do
And then he wondered as to why she had a cell phone
If she only seemed to answer when she
Was at home

Calling out to Ms. Wood
He cancelled the meetings for the remainder of his day
Rescheduling as many as he could for the following day
And dictating an email
To be sent as apology for such an action
Hoping that one's child was valid enough
As an excuse
He packed some work
Into the brown leather briefcase
That his parents had given him as a gift when he first
Came to the bank
But until this new promotion
Had been useless
For until now
All of his work could be accomplished
Within the eight hours that the bank had set aside
For his workday
The locks latched
He said goodbye to Ms. Wood
And with head slung low
His chin making a deep impression
On the space between the two points of his clavicle
Walked swiftly to the elevator
No one seemed to notice
Pressing the button for the garage
He descended into the dungeon of the building
Its few fluorescent lights
Humming and flickering as he located his black
Sedan among the other black sedans
Usually done by clicking the lock button
On the head of the key
Embarrassed by having to do so
He would always joke about it being an accident
Whenever others were around
But today the garage was empty
And no awkwardness came over him
At least not about the use of the key

II.

Though he tried to make sure to be there on time
Time never seemed to work well for him
When it came to picking up Izzy
On time
As today was like every other
Izzy was sitting, somewhat patiently
On the curb of the school's half-moon drive
Settling into the passenger seat
The click of the seat belt being buckled
The normal clue that the car could return to motion
Only this time
The click came at the same time as a great yawp
The yawp emanated from the lungs of Ms. Vasquez
The school vice principal
A morbidly obese woman
Which took some work
As she was inordinately tall
Much taller than Izzy or his father
She knocked on the passenger side window
Which Izzy tried to turn down
But which was locked
A disapproving look from both Izzy and Ms. Vasquez followed
At which point he mimed that he was sorry
Unlocked the window
And Izzy commenced lowering the glass back into the door frame

"Izzy can't just be left here this long after school, just waiting for your schedule to fit him in"
"my wife told me to be here at 4, and it is only 4:09, so my apologies"
"well she was wrong
Izzy has been on this curb
The last child waiting
Since 3:45"
"again, my apologies
But my wife was the one that usually picks Izzy up
But she is at the vet with our dog"
"oh… I am so sorry to hear it
I hope that the dog is feeling better soon
And please remember to get Izzy earlier"
"of course"

He reveled at how Ms. Vasquez's demeanor had changed
With the mention of the dog
He loved how his own problems would be excuses
But the dog
That was important
Or so others believed
And it was true
Rachel was in fact in the office with Dr. Hall
As they had been speaking
And while Dr. Hall was reassuring
Rachel that Felipe would be fine
And that she had not overreacted
That it was best to have brought him
If so concerned
It was now his turn
Upon mentioning Felipe's, as yet unknown to Izzy,
Visit
Izzy begged to know what was wrong
He had known of the lake, earlier
But why the veterinarian
He tried to tell Izzy that his mother was just overreacting
But it was of no use
Like mother, like daughter
Or in this case, son

Izzy demanded that they get home *post haste*
Obviously upset about Felipe
And obviously using that word a day calendar his father had bought him for his birthday
So the car was sped up
And a smile came across Izzy's face
As though this small victory would in fact make Felipe's prognosis
Better, if for no other reason than that it had happened
Having left the window down
After being spoken across
The wind stung Izzy's skin
But it did not bother him
As he knew it meant that he would soon be back with Felipe
And his mother
And those two were the ones that really understood him
40 in a 35 did not seem reckless
And it wasn't
At least it wasn't until he missed seeing ahead of time the stop sign
And while slamming on the brakes
Which fought to not lock up
The tires of the sedan hit a patch
Of black ice and by inertia alone
Moved into the intersection
Where it was met by a municipal garbage truck

The initial impact pushed the car
Against the direction of the tires
And west down Price Avenue
The sedan finally came to a complete stop
Pressed tightly against the front bumper of a parked car
The garbage truck had accomplished its stop much more quickly
And thankfully so
As the sedan had not much more room to move west
An unknown warmth started on the side of his face
To which he raised his hand to find blood flowing from
A rupture in the skin of his cheek
Not thinking it had been that devastating
He had not imagined there would have been blood
But now witnessing it
He turned to Izzy
To make sure he was alright
Metal from the door frame of the sedan
Had been reformed around the imprint
Of the garbage truck
And that new form
Had pierced through Izzy's chest
His eyes still open
The last look of life
His head flopped forward into his chest
He tried to shake him
To cajole him
But it was of no use
It was over
And as soon as it was over, the tears began to run in torrents down his cheeks
Catching some of the blood
And etching canyons in the blood as it mixed
And fell to his shirt

As the men from the garbage truck made it to the wreck
They yelled in
Not to move
As if that was much of an option
They yelled again
That it would be ok
That the ambulance was on its way
They not being able to see what he could see

He reached for his phone
Even over their yells for him to stop
He dialed his wife's number
Brought the phone to his ear
And waited the three rings, before it went to her voicemail

"you have reached Rachel's phone.
Sorry I am not able to answer your call,
But please leave a message after the tone
And I will be back with you shortly"

He tried his best to explain the accident
And that the ambulance was coming to get them
He did not mention that Izzy had died
That would be something he would need to tell her in person
He also mentioned that the nearest hospital was St. Vincent's
So that was probably the best place to start

"do you need to take that?"
"no, it is just my husband
Probably just calling to tell me that he has our son, and that they are on their way home
I will be home soon enough
No reason to call back"

The ambulance arrived first
But it mattered little
As it was not until the firefighters arrived
That the jaws of life could open
The mangled-metal mess that was
The black sedan
The blades ripping into the steel
Sheering in two what had once been one
Creating an opening in the passenger side
Much like one might open
A can of tuna

As soon as the metal crutch that held
Izzy erect was removed
He collapsed into a puddle of flesh and bone
Pronounced dead at the scene
He was strapped to a gurney
And placed neatly into the back of one of the ambulances
A white sheet adorning his body

Then came the work of removing his father
An easier task of engineering
But delicate
As his injuries could still sap the life from him
And as they strapped him to yet another gurney
He begged to ride with his son
Something that was not a possibility
Yet unimaginable
And impossible to get across to the man
As he cried and screamed for someone
Anyone to listen to him
They closed the double doors
Of the ambulance
As soon as the EMT was inside
He kept asking for his son
Not listening to what was being asked of him
Not caring
Only lost in the fact
The fact that his son
His only son
Israel
Was dead
This was not supposed to happen
Children bury parents
Not the other way around
So unbelievable is such a circumstance that he could not even think
Of the word for a parent that loses a child
If there even was a word
There was widow or widower
For those that lose a spouse
And orphan
For youngsters that lose their parents
But for him
For him no word existed
Nothing in the English language was prepared
For this loss of life; for this accident

"My phone! Where is my phone?"
"I don't know, sir"
"What do you mean you don't know?"
"I don't know… It was not on your person when I got to you"
"Damn it!"
"What's wrong?"
"I need to get a hold of my wife"
"We will figure that out later
You need to just stay calm
We're almost at the hospital
Just hold on"

Rachel pulled into the driveway
Felipe was not with her
She had been so distraught that Dr. Hall offered to keep him
For observation
The horn of her SUV chirped as she locked
The doors
She did not see their other car
Getting pissed
Wondering where they could be
It was almost 6
They better not be eating out
She had prepared a great dinner
And they were out eating at some damn restaurant
So upset
Rachel grabbed her phone
And dialed it blindly
No answer
No voicemail
He usually answered
Becoming livid, she called again
This time she got his voicemail

"Where the fuck are you?"
She said with the sweetest lilt in her voice
Continuing with that same volume
"You better not be at some restaurant
I told you I was preparing dinner at home tonight
So you better be home soon
Or I am going to fucking kill you
And I mean it this time, asshole"

Rachel ended the call
And noticed she had a voicemail from her husband
From his earlier call
No happier
She decided to listen
At least then, she would know where they were
She listened to it once
Looked at the time
Listened to it again
As her eyes clouded with tears
Unable to see her environment
She took the sleeve of her shirt
And wiped away the tears
Got back into her vehicle
And sped off to St. Vincent's hospital

Distraught
She left her car running
Door open
In the driveway of the emergency room
"Where is my son?" She screamed at no one in particular
Now finding the E.R. secretary
Inches from her face
Hands grabbing at the neck of her scrubs
"Where is my son, damn it!"
Before she got another word out
She was being pulled off by a security officer
Brought to the security office
She calmed down enough to explain
Who she was
And who she was there to find
A doctor was called
And the officer and Rachel waited for his arrival

III.

"where is my son?
Where is Izzy?
Why won't anyone tell me where he is?"
"you need to worry about yourself
And relax, sir
We will take care of your son"
"my son is dead
Tell me where you have him
I need to know
Has his mother arrived?"
"I don't know if she is here
But the boy
Your son
Izzy
He is in the morgue
Where he will remain until you are well enough to see him"
"was that so hard"

A huge spotlight came into focus over his bed
And the silent room began to buzz
With collective chaos
As if only he were calm
The masked faces
And uniformed uniforms
Made it hard to tell which were doctors
Which were nurses
Only the anesthesiologist
Was able to be discerned
And only because he placed a mask over the man's face
And whispered
In a controlled cadence
For the man to count back from ten
While taking deep breaths

Focus was lost
And then came back, but not in the operating room
Maybe the operating room had been a dream
Nightmare
Maybe it was all a bad dream
As he was not even a man any longer
But a boy
It was his sixth birthday
He knew that
Because he remembered the day well
As his grandfather, whose home the party had been at
Would be dead shortly after
And it was the only year he had hosted the party
As he could no longer travel
Not even the few miles across the city
To his grandson's
Suburban home
The hope being that removing their son from the neighborhood
The one in which his grandfather still resided
And the one in which both of his parents were raised
That he would have more opportunities
Which was a nice way of saying
That too many black families had moved into the old neighborhood
His parents would never say this
But his grandfather would bitch about it to anyone who would stay still long enough to listen
And many did
And agreed
And it would be a few years later
When the family decided it was time to get rid of the old home
That none of them wanted it
And that the neighborhood was a lost cause
They sold it
To a Vietnamese family

The Trongs
Who were living out their American dream
In a home that my family could no longer see theirs in

But that birthday was magic
And if it was again 1986
Then perfect
And if this was just a side effect of the anesthesia
Perfect
As this was a great day
It had been sunny and cool
The one cool day that anyone could recall of that summer
And he and his cousins would splash in and out
Of the kiddie pool
In its hard plastic mold
That his grandfather had purchased
Just for this day
And the joy in the old man's eyes
As he saw his nation giggling
And racing
Unafraid of the world around them
Unknowing of the cancer that was blackening his lungs
And happy to be with each other
As the next time they would do so
Would be his funeral
An idea that was not lost on him

The birthday boy closed his eyes to blow out all of the candles
All six of them
And he blew out his full lung capacity
Opened his eyes
And was thirteen rows back from his grandfather's casket
Unlike his birthday
He was alone
Not completely alone
But as a child alone
None of his cousins were allowed to make the trip
And many of his aunts and uncles had not been impressed that he had been allowed to come
But his parents did not parse words
Claiming that he knew what was going on
Which he did
And that keeping it from him only took away his chance to say goodbye
Everyone sat down
Which made the seating choice all the less rational
As there were nowhere near enough people to have filled the rows prior to the one
They had chosen to reside in
But there they were
Politely waiting for the service to begin
A plump, old man came to rest
Erect
Behind the pulpit or podium
Matters your belief as to whether you felt this was a religious or a public exercise
So it was a podium
To the young boy
And the old man opened the book in front of him to the marked page
And began to speak
In a voice not hallowed enough for just such an event
Religious or not

And it became clear
That the man had never met his grandfather
As it became a morose version of Mad-Libs
His grandfather's full name
Something he had not been called since his birth
Being glibly filled into the ominous blanks
On the sheet in front of him
The boy turned to his mother
Her tissue filled with lost opportunities to say "I love you"
And as he began to speak
He felt a pain in his side
He winced
And with eyes closed tried to will the pain away
As he had to tell his mother that he knew the truth of this ruse
But when he opened his eyes

He was in the lecture hall where he had taken freshman comp
The professor
A gorgeous grad assistant not much older than he
He loved this class
Not for the things he was not paying enough attention to to learn
But for the chance to see her ass length blonde hair sway as she walked up and down
The aisles, passing back the graded work
On this particular day, the girl next to him
A beauty in her own right
But a beauty he had not yet known, even though they had sat next to each other
For seven weeks
Struck up a conversation
Speaking of how the grading was bogus
How the girl (professor) had no clue as to what she was doing
And when he turned to defend his "professor"
He lost his train of thought
And could only nod in agreement

As this new woman
Was more beautiful than the one that he had allowed to cloud his thoughts for so long
She introduced herself
Rachel
He stammered out something close to a name
And the two continued to bitch
Back and forth
About this child professor and her inability to accomplish the work given her
It continued after class
When they drank coffee together
He never really liked coffee
And would never drink it of his own free will
But if it meant that she would continue to share his personal space
It was worth the burnt taste buds on the tip of his tongue
Ones that it would take four days to regain feeling
Or the acrid taste of the coffee in his throat
As he believed that he liked his coffee black
As god intended
And sure enough she stayed
And they began to talk about all sorts of topics
He just saying enough to keep her interest, but truthfully allowing her to lead the conversation
Two cups apiece later
They resigned to the dining hall
Where they both ate the spaghetti
And felt alone in the crowded room
The two would become inseparable
Something that would irritate each other's group of friends
The friends only truly bonding on their hatred of what their friends had become
But it didn't bother them
And a few weeks later they were boyfriend and girlfriend
Though they never took the titles
At that time they believed titles were much too possessive

They were deeply in love
Probably the deepest in love they had ever been or ever would be
At least with each other

That night
After the dining hall
They walked back to her dorm
Hand in hand
And as they approached the end of their day together
He leaned in
With all of his courage
And hope
And desire
And kissed Rachel on the cheek
Which was returned with a kiss on the lips
As Rachel felt the woman could make a move, too
And she did not want him to doubt her feelings
When the two could not figure out what was meant to occur next
Rachel excused herself
Something about needing sleep
And to do homework
And said they would see each other soon
And they did

He came to rest on his bed
Laid his head upon his pillow
Closed his eyes
And everything went black

It took a long time for the next picture to begin
As though the projectionist
Untrained
And unmotivated
And just barely nineteen
Had lost the next reel
The light flashed bright
The sound of the fan building in the background
And the flickering images finally finding cohesion

Institutional white walls
A window out onto the lake, the trees nude
And a breeze causing a ripple across the top of the otherwise glassy surface
The soundtrack crackles
And finally reaches full volume
He hears the action of the room
And turns just in time to see Izzy's head crown
A new sensation
As this was not in fact the view he had actually had on this day
He was to the side
Holding one of Rachel's legs, at a ninety degree angle
Pulling the knee back toward her chest
Just like the doctor asked
Hoping that what he was doing was of some help
Though from the expression on Rachel's face
He could have not been of much less help
He continued only for the reason
That if he were to stop
The doctor, too, would be upset
And he only cared to piss off one woman at a time
And if he did stop
What would he do
With his hands
With his body
With his voice
So as to not look even more useless than he already felt
And already assumed Rachel believed

When she was not pushing
Rachel kept her eyes closed tight
Wishing away everyone in the room
Wishing away her husband
Her mother
The three medical students that most likely could have painted
A portrait of her dilated vagina
If any had some artistic ability
And wishing away this child
That was taking his sweet ass time coming into being

Izzy finally arrived

And as he leaned in to kiss the young boy's freshly bathed head
It was over
The life history he was so enjoying came back to reality
And while he was still most definitely
Under
He knew that Izzy had died
That his boy no longer was of this world
And that he would still have to explain it
To Rachel

"Mrs. Leib?"
"yes" answered Rachel
"I am Dr. Simmons"
"and? Are you the one that is going to take me to my son, to my Izzy?"
"I will, ma'am, but…"
"but what?"
"we need to talk"
"about?"
"Izzy did not make it"
"what do you mean?"
"Izzy is dead"
"why didn't you save him? Why did you kill my son?
You are lying
Show me my son, you murderer!"
"ma'am, Mrs. Leib, he was pronounced at the scene
He was only brought here so that he and your husband would be at the same hospital"
Rachel closed her eyes
Tuned out the doctor
And only "returned" to the room
When he said he would take her to identify her son's remains
"you mean see my son"
The doctor didn't speak
He just held the door and led the way to the elevator
That descended three floors
And opened up onto a brightly-lit hallway
And led to a bank of plate-glass windows
Similar to the ones she had taken her family to
To see the newborn son
Her Izzy
Now the interior
Which had been lit to show off the newborns
Was dimmed to display those that remained to be identified
A metal exam table
Its edges obscured by a plain white sheet
That gave hints to the form of a small child

Rachel likened it to the furnishings of a summer home that had been closed up for winter
How the chairs and lamps had been draped by white sheets
To keep dust from settling into the fabric
And how death
Was now being kept from settling into the fabric of Izzy
There was still hope
Maybe it was not Izzy
Maybe they had brought in another boy
Maybe it was all just a misunderstanding
The doors swung open
The doctor sidled up to the head of the exam table
And with practiced hand
Pulled back the sheet to expose only the bust of the small child

Standing at the head of the exam table
Rachel looking down toward the foot
Felt there must have been some mistake
This was not her son
But on closer inspection
And when looking from a more natural angle
It was definitely Izzy
His face as angelic as she last could remember it
As though the accident
His death
Had caught him by surprise
And from the view she had been given, there was no clue as to why or how the boy could have died
The more ghastly image of the boy's torso
Being covered still
By the sheet
The injury
If seen would have eliminated any doubt as to the cause of death
But she loved the young doctor
For his measured response to her need

She could not have dealt with the visceral truth
But rather wanted to live in the bucolic lie
That he had just stopped breathing
Which was her blessing
A blessing
Not given to his father

The doctor asked
As was required, if this was in fact her son
To which she just nodded her head
Leaning forward to kiss his cold forehead
And to whisper in his ear
That she loved him
Not knowing if she had said so when she had dropped him off at school in the morning
Though he had yet to distance his love from his mother at this still young age
So she was hopeful that both had made mention of their love at their departure
But to be sure
She told him again
Hoping that he too
Like the comatose
Could hear
And when she felt sure that he knew her feelings toward him
She whispered a reassurance to him
That she knew how much he had loved her
Izzy was by no means a momma's boy
But he did love her
With all of his being
A love she returned equally
Resigned to her fate
She exited the room and headed back for the elevator
Followed gingerly by the young Dr. Simmons
And while sharing the elevator, it ascended toward the living
There was discussion about bringing Mrs. Leib to see her husband
Who should be in recovery by now
She declined
Making the excuse that she needed to call family
Which seemed rational

Rachel never made it to the recovery room
Well she did make it there, to the recovery room
She made it there
after her husband had been transferred

Rachel's cell rang nonstop
Making it feel, to her, as though she were one of those old time
Telephone operators
Picking up the line
But not being the one that people wanted
Sure they wanted her information
But their concerns were with the boy, now deceased
And her convalescing husband
No one seemed to worry about her injuries
As though they were blind
To her hurt
She sometimes passed the phone off to him
So that he could take on some of the responsibilities
But mostly it was her
Rachel
Having to relive the accident
And the loss
Almost hourly
If she was lucky
An accident that she has only pieced together slightly
On her own
But relayed with an authority that made many feel as though she may have been in the vehicle
Though they knew she had not

Eventually she stopped picking up the calls
With few exceptions
Her parents
The funeral home
People to whom she would not have to recall the details of her child's demise
For with so many retellings
The story began to fade from reality
And Rachel could not handle losing
Her son again

Her husband, bedridden
Was of little help
But was there to fill in details as she wanted them
Usually putting up her hand for him to stop
As in his desire to tell her everything
He never noticed the tears when they began to fall

Being that parents rarely bury children
It is obvious that the couple had no plans already hatched for a funeral
Had her husband died
Rachel would have been in better shape
As these discussions
While still premature
Had occurred with a frequency that she felt see could execute his desires
And she had shared enough
So she believed
That her husband should have been able to have done the same
Shit, they had already purchased side by side
Burial plots at the cemetery
The same cemetery at which his family had been buried for generations

It was this forethought that eased some of the decision making
about plans for Izzy's remains
as it was quickly decided that he would be buried in Rachel's plot
and that at the earliest convenience
they would look into buying an additional plot
he had offered up his plot
but Rachel had insisted
as she felt it would be only appropriate
and not wanting to make a fuss
or to cause pain at this time
he went along with her plan
and the cemetery sent out the crew
with the backhoe
to dig up the hardened soil

it was decided that the family would be the only ones to speak
at the service
which would be held at the graveside

he did not tell Rachel, again
of his grandfather's funeral
as she had heard the story before
and needed not an explanation for what seemed to be a genuinely fantastic idea

the day arrived
with little fanfare, outside of the family
a few of Izzy's classmates attended
with their families
the tiny pine box
stained cherry
stood still, suspended by straps over the six foot hole that had been dug in the cold, hard ground
the earth letting out its warmth
in a wafting cloud of steam
no one wanted to start
as starting would begin the end for Izzy
every person seeing each word spoken as one moment closer to the dirt
being shoveled on top of his casket
while heartfelt
the service seemed filled with clichés
as though Izzy was every kid
and no kid, at once
as though there was nothing unique or special
about the boy

his mother asked to speak last
a request quickly granted
so the time had come for his father to speak
of his son

"What does a man say about his son
To be honest
I thought
When I thought of my own life
And death
That it would be him
My Izzy
That would have the difficult task of figuring out
What to say
I hoped that he would remember me as a good father
A good man
Someone he could look up to
And come to when he needed answers
Instead it is to him that I come
For answers
Why me?"

He stared off into space
Lost in thought
Brought back by the clearing of
A throat
Whose he could not tell
That coupled with the tears starting to roll down his cheeks
And into his beard
Where they became lost
And would not fall
From his face
As though his sadness had been captured
Or rescued
He hoped the latter

"I keep asking myself
Why I was the one to survive
But in the end
That is not for me to know
It is just for me to accept
And hopefully
One day
Move on
But for today
For the time being
I want to tell you of my son

Izzy gave a shit
In a world where that stopped being a sign of being a good person
He would listen to song after song
Being played on the recorder
By the homeless man in the park near his school
And after each he would clap
And say that it was even better than the song before
And after each song in the man's repertoire
Izzy would place a dollar
Into the man's woolen cap
Placed conspicuously at the man's feet
Not because he felt sorry for the man
But because a man deserves payment for his work
And as it were
As long as Izzy stood
Hips swaying to the music
The man in the park made about ten dollars an hour

Another time
A classmate of his lost all of his belongings
In a house fire
That destroyed not only their possessions
But also the family's home
Knowing the difference between wants
And needs
Izzy asked if we could let the family
A girl and her two parents live with us
Izzy did many things well
But taking "no" for an answer was not one of them
We gave him reason after reason as to how it was not possible
That the family probably had friends
Or family to stay with
Izzy assured us of our fears
But that we were wrong
They had no one
And nothing
We started again
But he stopped us and went up to bed
When we finally headed to bed ourselves
Izzy was sleeping on an air mattress at the foot of our bed
I gently shook him awake
To which he said that he had found space
The next morning
Rachel called up the family of the girl
And had them moved into the house by the end of the day
That family stayed with us for three months
And are now as close as family
Because Izzy cared
I remembered telling him a week or so into all of this
How proud I was of him for doing this for his friend
To which he replied
That he had barely known the girl
But she seemed like she
And in turn her family needed help

Who takes a person like that away from the world
As much as that part of him is going to be missed
It is the things that he is going to miss
That kill me the most"

His tears returned
And without another word
He stepped out from behind the podium
And was quickly replaced by his wife, as if it were planned
As if choreographed
Though it was most certainly not

Much more composed
And not suffering
The survivor's guilt that had come to debilitate her husband
Rachel scanned the audience
The cemetery
And then began to speak

"I would like to take a moment to thank you all
For being here
For being with us
At this most difficult time
It is a testament to how much Izzy meant
To so many people

While I have my own collection of stories
Much like my husband
That show a glimpse of the man Izzy
Had already become
At such a young age
I feel it is the memories I am not going to be able to make with him
That hurt the most

I will not be able to talk to him about girls
About his first crush
About how he should share those feelings
Because one never knows what could be
To protect him through rejection
And build him back up for the next time
As there will always be a next time
To assure him that kissing gets better with time
And that the first time is always the yuckiest

I won't be able to see his nervous face
When he would have brought that first girlfriend home
To introduce her to us
Biting his lip in that cute way he did
Thinking no one ever noticed
Thinking he looked cool as a cucumber
While on the inside he was dying a slow death
Of nerves

I won't be able to bring him to Nelson's
To rent him a tux for his prom
Making sure he bought his date a corsage
Helping him tie his bow tie
Tweaking it
So that it looked perfect
And taking a slew of awkward
Pictures
That would line the mantel piece for years to come
One surviving
Even when he gets married
To a different person

I won't be able to wait for him
Outside of the maternity wing
When he bursts forth to announce the birth of his first child

I will not be a grandmother

I am no longer a mother

I no longer have my confidant

Or the best little spoon in the world

I have nothing

And I am nothing"

Her own mother came up behind her
And embraced her
As she collapsed into her arms
A bundle of tears
And pained sighs

Sitting back in the front row of chairs
Her son's casket seemingly levitating in the air
The mob of people
There to pay their final respects to the deceased
So many that the casket was unable to be seen
From the roadside
By their presence
It looked like a roving huddle of men
And women
Unable to look each other in the eye
Unable to put the syllables together in their mouths
To speak

If by magic
But actually by the cemetery staff waiting
In the wings
The casket
It's bright cherry/pine finish
Descended into the earth
To its final resting place
The straps recoiling back into the lowering apparatus
Those gathered said a few final prayers
And shoveled dirt onto the coffin
As was their custom

They came home to a house
Empty
Though filled with family
Friends and neighbors
All trying their best to fill the massive
Hole left by the loss
Of Izzy
With green bean casserole
And cholent
And other warm, hearty, filling
Foods that mean that the family could navigate through their bereavement
With full stomachs

Rachel's mother bunked in Izzy's bedroom
Filling his twin bed
As he had never been able to
Her silver hair contrasting the superman sheets
That stretched to the edges of the bed
She had hoped to stay on for as long as needed
To give Rachel a hand
But it became clear within the first few days
That Rachel; unlike her husband
Was not going to (need) use
The full seven days to wallow
But would instead lose herself in the dishes
Trying to remember to whom each dish belonged
So as to return them as soon as humanly possible
And much sooner than most had suspected
As her arrival at each of their homes was greeted by surprise
As joyful as it was
Surprise at her being up and around
Especially being that her husband had become a recluse
Only seen, not even in public, at the minyan
That took place in the living room of their three bedroom home at the end
Of a cul-de-sac
Had it not been for this twice daily excursion from his bed
Which usually required, at least to him, that he be presentable
He might have slipped into a Wilsonian slumber
Needing to be begged to see the light of day
Too weak to move forward
And needing to have his nails clipped
As though reverting to being an infant
In adult clothes
But it did not happen this way
But as soon as the last man left the house
He would return to the bedroom
Climb under the comforter
Close his eyes tight and try to sleep without dreaming
A more difficult task than he recalled it ever being before

IV.

Wanting to escape the dream was desired only because unlike the dream that stalked his adolescence, this one did not star a scantily clad young woman that had a penchant
For short, chubby, Semitic boys
This one
That played over and over again
Usually in slow motion
Was of the accident
The boy's hair blowing back in the chilled air that came through the opened
Passenger side window
The sedan hurtling through the semi-empty streets of town
Jazz blasting from the stereo system
A joyous shared moment
That led to the loss of sight
Of the intersection
And it's stop sign
A blur of red
That when seen some fifty feet ahead
Caused for an immediate application of the brakes
Which caught and released
And on the second catch, caught with it some black ice
Which sent the sedan aimlessly into the intersection
Where it was met by the imposing weight
Of the sanitation truck
He would see the steel frame of the sedan
Morphing shape around the front end of the truck
And the entrance of a piece of the bent frame
Into the torso of Izzy
And as the blood began to evacuate his chest
The dream would rewind
And begin again
Sleep was impossible
But being awake was even more difficult
He laid there
Eyes closed
Exhausted

Day became night
And night, day
And the ancient chants became his only escape those first seven days

The days turned to weeks
And light began to return to his life
And the days became more bearable
He and Rachel feel back in love
Or at least that was how it felt
To each of them
A closeness
That they had once known
That was again kindled
And while both felt great comfort in this
It felt not worth the cost
But neither wanted it to end
And so the thoughts of its origins
Faded
And the couple became one

They would go on dates
To the movies
Where the dark of the theater allowed each to feel safe
And free to just be
Rachel resting her head on his shoulder
And a few times
When the movie did nothing for her
She fell asleep
And here
In the vacuum of the movie theater
She did not have to dream
And could actually rest
He would turn his head over to look at hers
To see if she were asleep
And if so
He would sweetly kiss her forehead and turn back to the screen
Where he would escape
As the weeks had seen a loss in frequency
Of his recurring dream
And restful sleep became not a certainty
But much more certain than the recent past

Many of these movies would be preceded by a dinner at a nice cafe
Or restaurant
Something one was not able to do with an eight year old
As Izzy had been a finicky eater
This was brought up one night
And actually brought smiles to their faces
A happy memory
A memory that had not caused tears
They were not forgetting the young boy
Just successfully moving forward
Not on

They could go to the Thai restaurant they had loved
When they were in college
But that never seemed possible
With a child in tow

They would take off in the middle of the week
And take vacations in the middle of the school year
And not think twice
As they had once had to be so mindful of
And on one of those escapes
They took a room
Ordered food to the room
A bottle of champagne
And cuddled up under the sheets
They touched for the first time in months

Sure they had shared a bed this whole time
But had been much less intimate
Until this night

They made love
And it was passionate
Passionate like it had not been in years
And collapsing in a pile in the middle of the bed
He held her tight to his naked body
Her naked form melting into his
As though one body
And it was at that moment
That they both knew it was over

They barely spoke the next morning as they ate in the hotel lobby
Returning to the room to pack up their things
Load the car
And head back home
A three hour trip
That was punctuated by silence
Arriving home
They went on with their own routines
And the dates stopped
And no longer did they go as frequently to the movies
And if they did
Rachel never again fell asleep on his shoulder
A quite rage built for days
Until he made what would be looked back at
As the fatal mistake
Instead of waiting for her to explode in speech
He asked her what was the matter

Her eyes
So distant became engulfed in rage as she turned to him
Her face taut with disgust
"You know why?"
"But I don't"
"You killed my son!"

"excuse me!"

"you heard me!
You killed my son!!
The only thing I had in this world"

"first of all
I did not kill your son
Last time I checked
He died in a fucking car accident"

"that you caused"

"oh, that's right
I remember that now
I willed that fucking garbage truck to crash into my son
I asked the driver to be driving as fast as he could
And I would purposely slide into the intersection
Assumedly out of control
What kind of fucking monster do you think I am?"

"the kind that takes away my son
From me"

"of course
You are the only one who lost anything
My son is still here
I forgot"

"don't mock me"

"I am not mocking you
I am just trying to understand
How you lost everything
And I am the sole cause of all of that loss
And how you seem to feel as though I lost nothing in this tragedy
As though my son did not die
As though I did not have to be there when he screamed out in pain
And all I could do was tell him it would be all right
As though I wanted to be free of him
As though I lost nothing
I saw the life leave his eyes
I heard his soul escape his body
And I got to do all of this
With excruciating pain
Both for our loss
As it is our loss
And for my own pain and injuries
Which are obviously lessened
By the loss of Izzy
But which I did live through, too"

"stop being the fucking martyr!"

"are you fucking kidding me?
I am sorry that you lost your whole life
Makes me feel great about my place in your life
As if I did not already know where I ranked
But I was there
I was driving
I had to live through the gruesome
Mess that was his death
And I suffered, too
And if that counts for nothing to you
Then so fucking be it
But don't come around me fucking crying about how you lost your reason
To live
And tell me I'm the fucking martyr
Look in the goddamn mirror, bitch
If I am a martyr
I learned how to be one from the very best"

"you are such a fucking asshole
And so fucking self-righteous
And yes you were driving
And it is that reason that I fucking blame you
If it were me
This would not have happened"

"oh, I see
Little miss perfect can stop nature"

"don't patronize me"

"I am not, and will never, patronize you
But realize that I live with that thought each day
And you throwing it in my face does not make it hurt less
And you are not perfect
And neither am I
But I get to be the lucky bastard
Who was driving
And have an accident
And yes I wish I could take it all back
But I can't
And the sooner you fucking get that through your head
That I didn't do this on purpose
Which I most certainly didn't
The easier this is going to be on us"

"you don't deserve for this to be easy
On you
You killed my son
My son
I am the one who gave birth to him
I am the one who suffered with him
I am the one who always made him better
I am the one who he came to when he was lost
And you have taken all of that away from me
And now I am just left with you!"

"left with me?!
Am I that useless to you
And I am just left with you
But you do not see my complaining
You don't see me screaming
Yelling
Crying about what I lost
Because we lost
We lost a son
Not me
Not you
But I guess that is lost on you
I guess I am nothing to you"

"that isn't what I said
And you fucking know it"

"do I"

"stop interrupting"

"you interrupted me
I listened to your shit
You listen to me now
Do you think you are the only
One in pain
As if I am
All happy here
Not feeling the loss
The loss that is only yours
Supposedly
But it was me that had to watch him die
It was me that had to witness the end
And I get to be the one that already feels
As if I am to blame
I can kill myself inside all by myself
I don't need your fucking help
Never have
Never will
And here I was thinking
Thinking that you cared still
That this still meant something
But you are just
Keeping up appearances
Letting my family
Your family
Our friends
Think as though we are stronger than ever
That our love is solid
When really
Really all you want is for me to die
And for your son to be back
And if I could give you that I would
I really would
Because being dead would be better than living like this

Don't fucking try to walk out on this conversation
You started this
Don't back down now
Now is the time
Say it
Fucking say it"

"say what?"

"that you wish it had been me
That if I were dead you would have been fine
You would have moved on
That you would not be here blaming Izzy, or anyone else, for my death
That you wish you were free of me
That you do not love me
You don't
Do you?"

"you know that answer"

"I want to hear you say it
I want you to have the fucking balls to come out and fucking say it
Tell me you do not love me anymore
Maybe ever
Tell me it's over
Tell me you wish I was dead"

"I do
I wish it was you who were dead
That it was Izzy that I had back
I don't love you
And probably have not loved you in a very long time
But was never strong enough to say it
But that does not matter now
Because here we are
Alone
Together"

"you don't speak for me
I do love you
And while it would be great to be whole again
I do not need that to love you
I did not stay for Izzy
I stayed all these years
Because I loved you"

"the fuck you do"

She storms out the door
And speeds off into the distance
In her car
Leaving her husband
Alone
Dead
Unable to understand what just happened
Not that she really knows what just happened
Playing it over and over
In her mind
Trying to piece together
What was said
What was meant
What was truth
And what was said just to hurt
She grabs her phone and tries to call him
No answer
Pissed
She speeds on

"where the fuck is the printer"
Screaming to no one in particular
Wanting an answer but knowing that there is no one here to give it to him
He moves around the house
With an exaggerated limp
Trying not to use the cane at home
He knows that it lives
If a plastic box filled with electronics and ink
Can actually live
In a closet, somewhere in the house
He peaks his head into his son's room
Hoping he will not have to enter completely
Not wanting to disturb the contents
Tiptoeing in
He opens slightly the closet door
And sure enough
On the shelf above the hangers
Lives the printer
Holding himself up best he can
He wrestles with the printer
Knocking down most of the other inhabitants of the shelf
But finally succeeding in getting the printer
Carrying it back to the desk
Placing it down
He realizes that he has none of the cords
Another voyage of discovery
As they are not present in Izzy's closet
Searching desperately for them
Finding them in a drawer inside of the pantry
The last place he looked
But like last places looked
It was where what he was looking for was found
Connecting the printer
He goes about printing the document that he has been working on

Spewed from the printer
He places the document on the keyboard of the laptop
Only to realize that nothing is printed
Upon the paper
No ink
What are the fucking chances
Too upset to continue
He decides to leave the document open on the laptop
Using the unprinted upon paper in his hand
To scribble a note to read the screen

His right palm planted firmly against the wall
Of the corridor
He pushes off the wall
Shuffles his feet a few steps
And plants his palm again
That right palm
Against the corridor wall
Repeating this process
Mechanically
Another three times before he reaches the bathroom
He removes his pants
And sits on the toilet
The whole time
He stares back over at the vanity, upon which is the shaving set that Rachel
Had bought him two years ago for his birthday
It was said to have been from Izzy
But really
Rachel

It was a replica antique set
With the cup
The lather brush
And a single-blade razor
He studied the razor
Reading every detail of the machinated design
The shine still present
As he had never used the set
Liking the aesthetic
Of it more than its possible functionality
Wiping
And then flushing the toilet
He continued to eye the razor as he washed his hands
Which more resembled a surgeon scrubbing in for surgery than
A traditional after shit washing
His eyes never leaving the razor

Fully robed, again
He went off looking for a small Phillips head screwdriver
The kind one uses to tighten the screws of their glasses
Searching the junk drawer in the kitchen
As that had proved to be its home so many times before
And it was again this day
The tool in hand
He headed back to the bathroom
Flipped the switch that lit up
The vanity
His pale, stubble covered face coming into harsh focus
Hand reaching for the razor
And as he touched the metal of the handle
A car horn sounded
Rachel had returned
And this first attempt was thwarted, as he had not the energy
Or the fortitude to go through with it
If he might be able to be saved
It must be certain
She called to him as she entered the house
He was in the living room
Searching through an out of control pile of dvds
That they called a collection
She kissed him on the cheek
Said nothing
And he located the film he wished to watch
Placed it in the player
And went about cozying up in the couch
Under the blanket
As the previews
Long out of date
Played across the screen
Rachel yelled back, asking what it was that he was going to watch
"the Last Emperor", he replied with little enthusiasm
She made no retort
As she hated the film

And he knew it
But she did not want to have to speak to him any more than was necessary
So she breathed in deeply
Thought about telling him to enjoy it
But knew it would come out wrong
So she grabbed a book from her bedside table
Got under the covers of the bed, and read, as the dog curled up
By her side

By the time the film had finished
Four hours later
She had fallen asleep
And he was hungry
He went to see if she wanted anything to eat
But seeing her
Book splayed on her chest
He just stood there
Unsteadily
For a moment
Before removing her glasses to the low growl of her dog

The next few days went back to routine
But the feeling behind the routine
That had returned in the weeks after the accident
Was now gone
And unknown to the pair
Was lost forever
They tried to fake it
But she could always tell when he was lying
And though she did not know
He had always been able to discern when she was faking it
Whether it was a feeling of love
Or the orgasm he somehow always was able to give her
And just like those orgasms
Her dialect changed when she said loving things to him now, as if they were not natural
And she, and he, had to work hard
To kiss
Or touch each other's hands
And when they did by chance touch moving throughout the house
One or the other, and even sometimes both, would jump back
As though shocked by the physicality of it all
The hours of this charade slowly became fewer and fewer
With his recuperation
And return to work
He had been working quite successfully from home for a while
And the bank had been fine with him taking more time at home
But this fully-staged play at home
Took too much out of him
And with her always at home
It was too much
So when his doctor cleared him
He was at work that afternoon

He had actually come to the doctor's appointment in a new suit
And with his leather briefcase
Just in case
Phoning home to tell Rachel
Who was floored by such a rapid change of events
But also welcomed the move
As she missed her time
Alone

The thoughts of killing himself
Subsided, but still poked their head out every now and again
Not wanting him to forget about them
But in no rush for him to act them out
He found more work to do
Even when it did not readily exist
So that his hours at the bank grew and grew
Which was good for his mental health
And did not seem to faze Rachel
Who barely recognized his disappearance
Her shock came more from his existence within the home
Never aware of his presence until in it

Each day his secretary would wave
From the other side of the glass
As she left for the day
And he continued to pound the keys of his laptop
Ms. Wood, his secretary, always thought
Of him as a workaholic
She left late
But never before her boss
And without fail he would arrive before her in the morning
Always pounding on that keyboard
He must have had a continual pile of work
So she thought
But in fact
Most of that typing was a continuous rewriting
Of the six or seven draft documents
He had created
To tell Rachel
To tell the world
Of his death
His suicide
Feeling that one form letter would not work for all audiences
And knowing that certain items must be left
Off of certain letters
And greater details given to those closest to him
Delicate for his mother
Straightforward to his father
And blunt to Rachel

He would wave back
To Ms. Wood
And yell
Hoping to pierce the forced quiet of the panes of glass
To express to her
His desire that she have a great evening
But she never seemed to hear
Either too polite to scream back
Or the glass proved
To actually be impenetrable
Which did not seem possible
As conversations within his office always seemed more hushed than necessary
The reasoning always being that one did not know
Who might happen by
But scream as he tried
Ms. Wood would not know
Would never know
exactly how much he cared

Back to the screen of his laptop
He commenced editing the letter to his mother
Wanting her to know that what happened
Had nothing to do with her
That she had been the best mother a boy could have had hoped for
That she had given him all of the love
And support
That he needed
And that he knew how much this was going to hurt
But the pain of his loss
His losses
Was too much to bear any longer

The irony was lost
On him
He no longer
Could see the forest for the trees

He casually caught the time
On the screen of the laptop
And realized he had spent enough time
At work
On his mother's letter
And that Rachel must have fallen asleep
By this time
He pulled on his winter parka
How he hated to be so bundled up
And made it to the garage
To find that his was the only car
Left in the hulking structure
Pulling onto the avenue ahead of him
It too was empty
Lest for the few men and women
Huddled in jackets, scarves, and hats
Making their ways to the myriad
Pubs and bars
Of the financial district
Unfortunately
He did not wait long enough
For as he pulled into the driveway
At home
He saw the living room of the house
Was still illumined
And smoke wafted from the chimney
Turning off the car
He sat in the dark garage for a few minutes
Not wanting to disturb the beauty of his day
Not wanting to have to defend his life
To his wife
In the absence of their son's

He had spent too much time in the car
Knowing any further length of time
Would result in a visit from his wife, and a less than genuine inquiry
To his situation
Not wanting that
He unbuckled and took the few steps up into the house
A bottle of wine
Mostly gone
Littered the island in the recently-remodeled kitchen
Felipe sauntered across the tile floor
Sleepily greeting his "master"
Both knowing it is more a courtesy
Not a longing
Neither wanting to have their behavior dissected
By the lady of the house
He gently scratched behind the dog's ears
And walked past him into the living room
Only to be accompanied in short order
Rachel was slouched in an armchair
One of those upholstered in a deep cherry leather
With tacks giving a design to the face of the arms
Placed recklessly in front of the fire
Not for the cozy look of it
But for the utility
A wine goblet cradled
In her upturned palm
The dregs of the last glass
Slowly trying to stain the crystal
He removes the glass
To return it to the kitchen
And as soon as her grip is loosened from it
Her hand curls up into her chest
And he pulls the blanket
That draped low across her body
Up over her shoulders
Tucking it in slightly

Hoping it may stay the rest of the night
Stoking the fire
He kisses softly Rachel's forehead
Before placing the goblet in the sink and walking slowly off to bed
Not wanting to make a sound
Maybe he could still escape her inquisition
Each stair a nerve wracking evolution
Felipe stared up at him
Curled at her feet
In front of the fire
He made it to his bed
His son's bed
But the one he had come to use
And warmed himself under the blanket
Between the ice cold sheets
Curling up in the fetal position
His hands jammed between his thighs for warmth
Thinking of the fire
So close
But not worth the risk

V.

His alarm filled the room
With music
Loud enough to usually wake him
But not this day
Instead
He had the pleasure of waking up to Rachel violently shaking his arm
A look of complete displeasure on her face
As if
She could not see all he had done for her the night before
But unwilling to poke the bear
He acknowledged her disapproval
And with haste made his way to the shower
And got ready for another day of work
Ms. Wood had a broad smile on her face
As he arrived to his office
He thought to ask why
But he loved it too much to overanalyze it
He opened up his laptop and got back to work
Looking over the changes
To his mother's letter
Satisfied
He opened the file that contained his father's version
And returned to work on this next opus

The phone rang on his desk
It never rang
He was not even sure that anyone knew the number
It did not appear on his business cards
And if he did give out a work number
It was Ms. Wood's line
So she could run interference for him
With the caller
But this was a direct call
Unsure of what to do
He let it ring through to his voicemail
No matter whom the caller was
He could always manufacture an excuse as to why it went to voicemail
Checking the time on his laptop
He went back to the letter
While he waited out five minutes
Figuring the message would be available to listen to by that point
As soon as his glance caught the completion
Of the waiting period
He picked up the receiver
And dialed the mailbox
It took a moment for the voice to come to life
But as soon as it did
He knew it was Rachel who had called
Who else would it have been
Upset and accusatory
She went into a rant of how he was hiding
And using work as an escape
But this soon subsided and completed
With notice that she was taking Felipe
To the vet for boarding
And then would be hitting the road to spend a long weekend with friends
She only said that she was leaving today

And that she would be back sometime during the day on Monday
Hanging up the phone
He felt lighter
He could return home
To his bed
To the comfort he had left
And he could finally recharge
Through all of her hate
She had given him a gift
Rachel had unknowingly given him a home
What she needed to flee the house to find
Excited
He typed a few new lines in the letter to his father
Shut the screen of the laptop
Put on the jacket to his suit
Whispered he was heading to an early lunch in Ms. Wood's ear
And whistled as he walked to the bank of elevators
Ready to descend
And live

He enjoyed a perfectly seasoned steak
A pint of some local brew
And the leisure of being alone
Eating at the bar
He traded idle chat with the bar tender
Speaking of the cold weather
Why either of them continued to live in such a place
With such horrible winters
About this weekend's ball games
About the droning sound of Christmas carols
Where either of them found themselves
Actually causing the bar tender to tune in a jazz station
As they had noticed the irony of the carols
As they spoke of their shared disdain for them
He finished the last bite of his steak
Leaving the dregs of the beer in the bottom of the pint glass
Wished his new friend a great weekend
And left him a hefty tip
On the polished pine of the bar
Waving back at the bar keep
As thanks came for the gratuity

Taking a longer route back to the bank
His cheeks were a rosy hue by the time he reentered the office
Ms. Wood just stared
Slack jawed
"Don't worry, Ms. Wood, all is well"
He sat in his chair
Opened the laptop
And looked over the type in front of him
Reading each line with clarity and care
Wanting to choose the perfect word
A refined diction that his father would respect
Feeling that he had done enough
He saved the letter
Looked in the memory for the next to work on
And came to the realization that he had completed this most morbid of tasks
Feeling accomplished
He packed his laptop into his leather attaché
And got ready to leave
Stopping by his secretary's desk
To give her the rest of the day off
Shocked
And not wanting him to change his mind
She closed out of what she was doing
Gathered up a few things
And walked out the door alongside her boss
Just to make sure this was no ruse
Wishing each other a good weekend
They got into their respective cars
And headed out into the cold afternoon
And to their homes
Ms. Wood stopping off for a bit of shopping
As he sped home
Alone

He started a roaring fire
Setting up his chair in front of the fireplace
The ottoman placed just close enough to feel the warmth
Without the threat of catching fire
Pouring himself a scotch
He loosened his tie
Found that comfortable spot in the chair
Plopped his feet
One crossed over the other
Onto the ottoman
Closing his eyes
Grabbing his drink by muscle memory
And taking a long sip
As the crystal pressed tightly to his lips
Warmed completely
He let out a sigh
And released a great deal of weight
From off of his shoulders
He felt alive

VI.

Having reached such a perfect relaxation
He had fallen asleep in the chair
Only waking to the chirps of what few birds were left this time of year
Bleary eyed, he covered his eyes from the light
And stretched out the rest of his body
He headed to the bathroom
Taking a steaming hot shower
The water streaming down his face
Melting the aches of a night asleep in the armchair
Toweling off his fade
And wrapping the damp towel around his waist
An unnecessary modesty
But one that he had committed to rote
Entering his closet
He began looking around for some relaxed clothing
Stepping on a stool
He rummaged through lesser used clothing
That littered the shelf that worked its way around the entire
Space of the closet
Reaching the next pile of sweaters
He noticed
By touch
That they were stacked on top of a box
Removing the box
A wooden box that was foreign to him
He took it over to the bed
Opened the lid
And surprisingly found that its contents were a handgun
A revolver
With an additional supply of bullets
Copper in hue
Uninterested any longer in finding clothing
He took the box downstairs
And set it on the dining room table
Sitting down in front of it
He reopened the top

And just stared at the metal
And how the light glinted off of it
Letting his fingers trace over the figure of the revolver
He lifted it from the box
Feeling its weight in his hand
Seeing that it was in fact loaded
The filled chambers staring back at him
He aimed at the leafless oak in the dining room window
Making a sound with his mouth
Like he had as a little boy
When he shot dead the Indians
With his handgun
Quite literally made with his hand
His thumb the hammer
And his middle finger the trigger

And like those days
He held the barrel of the revolver against his temple
It weighed heavier against his skin
Than had his index finger
His finger playfully toying with the trigger
Wanting it to feel real, but not wanting for the possibility of an accident
As his finger rested substantially on the trigger
For the first time
The house phone rang
Startled
He struggled not to pull the trigger
Out of reflex
But could not keep himself from doing so
The trigger came close to flush with the grip
Of the revolver
The hammer fell
And the chamber rotated sixty degrees
After the escape of the bullet

The sound of the explosion
Deafened the ring of the phone
Which rang another couple of times before the caller gave up
The bullet quickly pierced the skin of his face
Tearing a hole in layer after layer
Moving through muscle and bone
And meeting little resistance as it
Dissected his brain
Blood flowing in the exact opposite direction
Of the bullet
He did not feel a thing
Shock set in quickly
Followed promptly by death itself
Most of the carnage taking place after
He had expired

His lifeless form crumpled to the table
First his hand losing control of the revolver
Which came to rest with a thud
On the carpeted floor
Accidentally discharging another bullet
This one
Slicing through the air and finding a final resting place
In the dense wood grain of the china cabinet
The inertia of the original bullet
Moving his head to the left
And forward
His forehead coming into contact with the table
With great force
Creating a laceration that allowed for his blood to escape
Even faster
Having two routes
Instead of one
This secondary route
With less traffic
As the flow had started to taper prior to its opening up
But the blood that had taken the alternate route
Had found the few porous sections of the wood
And had begun to soak into the grain
Making the table unable to be salvaged
A complete loss

Rachel hung up the phone
Taking a deep breath
Which she held for a ten count
She picked the receiver back up
And proceeded to call the office
Where the phone echoed off of the glass walls
Of his office
Creating a sound loud enough for all to have heard
Had anyone been in the office
But as it was in fact empty
This call ended in the same result
Frustration
She bitched about how inconsiderate he was to have not even made an effort to pick up the phone
Not wanting him to get the better of her
She went back to her life
Satisfied will the idea of just calling later
And at that time
Ruining the life of the person who deserved it

She called back
Again
No answer

The blood pooling
On the table
Around the gaping wound

She tried his cell
Which vibrated in the pocket of his pants
Until the number of tries was met
And his voicemail answered
"Sorry I can't come to the phone right now
But if you leave a brief message and a number
I will get back to you soon
Thanks"
Seething in anger
Her teeth grinding one on the other
She spoke in a tone
Completely absent of love
Through her tightly clenched jaw
"First of all
You know exactly who this is
You asshole
And what the fuck makes you think that you do not have to answer
My calls
I am done spending my time on you
I can't fucking believe this
Answer the damn phone
Fine
You better hope you are dead
Because otherwise I am going to fucking
Kill you
Call me
Love you"

That last phrase escaped her mouth
Involuntarily
She tried to suck it back in
Like a long flaccid piece
Of angel hair spaghetti
But no matter how hard she tried
She could not unsay it
Even if she did not mean it
Anymore

A few moments of awkward silence
And she ended the call
Upset that now he would think that she cared
Or that they would need to talk about the silence
That she had left at the end of the message
Either conclusion
Or both
Hardened her heart even more
Placing the phone by her side
She ordered another
Drink
A vodka cranberry

Hours passed
With no reply
Every so often she would check
Her phone
Make sure it still had life
Double check that the ringer was in fact on
Search for the phantom missed call that she was sure must have come
Three more hours passed
No longer wanting to just complain
She now wanted to crucify this man
For the way she was being treated
As though she were an afterthought
Slowly dialing the numbers
As if the deliberateness of the action
Would cause a different outcome
When she pressed call
It rang
But she expected no one to answer on the first ring
As there was a chance that that ring only occurred on her end
But the second should be the first chance
For success
But it proved naught
On the third ring
A woman's voice came to life on the other end of the line

Rachel thought that she must have dialed the wrong number
Even though she had been so deliberate
She must have pressed a wrong number
She held the phone away from her ear and read the number
On the illumined screen
Number by number she studied it
Each number was correct and correctly placed
In order
By the time she returned to the line
It was dead
Thoughts of other women
Of wild weekends
Of infidelity
Flooded her brain
Leaving in its wake damp remains
That quickly began to foster the moldy
Beginnings of jealousy
Rachel's finger quickly navigated to the recently dialed number
Pressing it
It again rang
And this time, when the woman answered
She had a response

www.ingramcontent.com/pod-product-compliance
Lightning Source LLC
LaVergne TN
LVHW091308080426
835510LV00007B/406